The Huguenots: The History and Legacy of the French Protestants and Their Religious Conflicts with the Catholics

By Charles River Editors

A cross used by the Huguenots

About Charles River Editors

Charles River Editors is a boutique digital publishing company, specializing in bringing history back to life with educational and engaging books on a wide range of topics. Keep up to date with our new and free offerings with [this 5 second sign up on our weekly mailing list](), and visit [Our Kindle Author Page]() to see other recently published Kindle titles.

We make these books for you and always want to know our readers' opinions, so we encourage you to leave reviews and look forward to publishing new and exciting titles each week.

Introduction

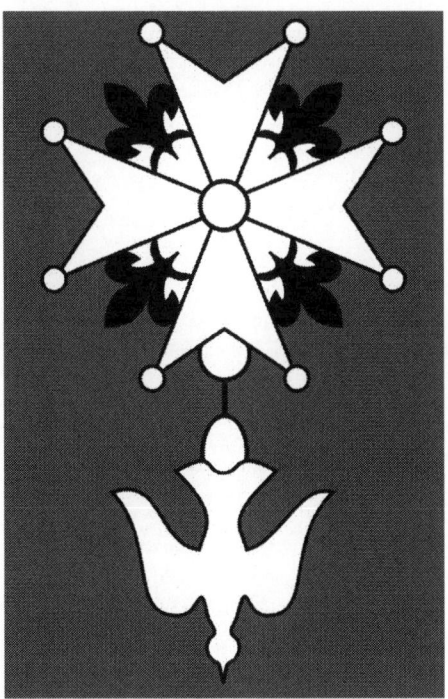

A cross used by the Huguenots

The Huguenots

"A dog barks if he sees someone attacking his master; I would indeed be cowardly if, seeing the truth of God thus attacked, I played the mute, without saying a word." – John Calvin to Marguerite, Queen of Navarre, April 1545

In the 16th century, corruption, debauchery, and the general perversion of ethics were running rampant within the Roman Catholic Church. The public began to grow leery of the crooked church, and soon, they could no longer bite their tongues. Among the church's most vocal opponents was Martin Luther, whose publication of the 95 Theses gave rise to the Protestant movement.

This reformed brand of Christianity gradually spread throughout Europe, planting flags across the continent. France was among the first to latch onto the movement, and these new-wave Protestants became known as the "Huguenots." The exact origins of the Huguenot name is still disputed to this day, but most historians have agreed it is a French and German translation of the Swiss-German term, "eidgenossen," meaning "oath-fellowship." The Huguenots mostly resided in the southern regions of France, along with the northern regions of Normandy and Picardy. They shared quite a few similarities with the Protestant Walloons, who lived in what is now Belgium, but the two groups were unique communities. Even so, both groups frequently convened to worship together as refugees.

The Huguenots, whose belief system incorporated a blend of unorthodox Waldensian and Calvinist teachings, continued to bloom, which did not sit well with the authorities. Critics attributed the rise of Protestant-led riots to the no-good Huguenots. The Huguenots were known iconoclasts who rejected statues, paintings, idols, and other religious images, as often seen in the numerous statues and stained glass artwork in Catholic churches. Across Europe, rebellious Protestants seized Catholic churches and swiped all heretical images, destroying them with axes and hurling them into roaring bonfires. The string of ambushes included the 1562 Looting of the Churches in Lyon, which were followed by similar attacks in Zurich, Copenhagen, Geneva, and many more.

Even in the face of persecution, the Huguenot influence gained momentum in France. A year before the looting, 2,500 Protestant congregations had already been established across the nation. The Huguenots held their services behind the curtains of secrecy, most commonly in the dead of the night. Some historians believe this clandestine operation could be related to the origin of their name. "Le roi Huguet," meaning "King Huguet," referred to purgatory spirits who haunted the living at night. Their perseverance eventually caught the eye of a pallid-faced Venetian ambassador, who purportedly warned his Catholic superiors that "3/4 of France was contaminated with the heretical doctrine."

The Huguenots' burgeoning power and alleged attempts to infiltrate the world of politics soon alarmed the French authorities. They suspected that these Huguenots were low-profile republicans, involved in a terrible conspiracy to conjure up an uprising to overthrow the monarchy and re-brand France as a federal state. The royal government of France would attempt to tread lightly in the beginning, keeping their hands clean on neutral grounds, but a nightmare was about to unfold.

In the 1560s, French authorities called for the violent and bloody persecution of all Huguenots. This hostile period of 36 years, fraught with conflict, upheaval, and civil vendettas between the Huguenots and Catholics, is now known as the "French Wars of Religion," or simply, the "Huguenot Wars." A short stretch of peace would later emerge as the wars began to wind down, but bloodshed was once again resurrected by rebellions brought forth by the persecuted.

The Huguenots: The History and Legacy of the French Protestants and Their Religious Conflicts with the Catholics examines the events and cast of characters that led to the persecution of the religious minority and their battles with the Catholics, one of the most fascinating chapters in all of French history. Along with pictures depicting important people, places, and events, you will learn about the Huguenots like never before.

The Huguenots: The History and Legacy of the French Protestants and Their Religious Conflicts with the Catholics

About Charles River Editors

Introduction

   The Seeds of Reformation

   Royals vs. Huguenots

   King Louis XIII

   The First Rebellion

   Take Two

   The Final Stand

   Online Resources

   Bibliography

Free Books by Charles River Editors

Discounted Books by Charles River Editors

The Seeds of Reformation

Towards the 16th century, the introduction of the Protestant Reformation in Europe threatened to crack the foundations of the Roman Catholic Church. The restless public began to distrust the church and shunned them for their corrupt ways, accusing the Catholics of consciously wandering away from God's light. Perhaps one of the most audacious abusers of authority was the holy Pope Leo X himself. Upon entering his papacy, he was supposedly quoted as saying, "Since God has given us the papacy, let us enjoy it."

Pope Leo X

Pope Leo was often commemorated as a liberal pacifist with a tremendous heart. That said, he also gained notoriety for his insistence on a lavish and sumptuous lifestyle. As he began to warm up the seat of his papal throne, he rolled up his sleeves and took it upon himself to reinvent the Catholic empire. His first order of business was to speed up the construction of St. Peter's Basilica. The pope then began to splurge on sculptures, paintings, intricate stained glass masterpieces, and other costly artwork. His frivolous granting of bishopric positions to his relatives only aroused more grumbling from outsiders. He was repeatedly warned about his financial habits, but his reckless spending sprees continued. Within 2 years, he had exhausted the papal treasury.

The pope was in a pickle; he needed to find a way to scrounge up the remaining half of the bill for the unfinished basilica. And so, a special tax known as an "indulgence" was created. For a fee, the grieving could bring their deceased loved ones out of Purgatory, and soar past those on Heaven's waiting list. For an even heftier price, one could purchase their own spots in Heaven in advance.

Meanwhile, Pope Leo supposedly harbored a twisted friendship with Cardinal Albert of Brandenburg. At 23, Albert reigned as both Archbishop of Magdeburg and the Administrator of Halberstadt, which was traditionally against canon law. Yet in this climate of corruption, this, as with many other laws, was swept under the rug. When the post of Archbishop of Mainz became up for grabs, Albert yearned to add a third title to his repertoire, an ambition hampered by the fact his funds were also looking a little dry. Albert succeeded in obtaining an IOU from Jakob Fugger, an extremely wealthy Austrian merchant and reported "florin multimillionaire." After securing the loan, Albert paid Leo the staggering entrance fee and was declared the Archbishop of Mainz. Soon after, the Pope sanctioned the practice of indulgences in Germany. Johann Tetzel, a Dominican monk, was appointed Germany's commissioner of indulgences, acting as a traveling salesman of sorts. Half the profits derived from the indulgences would be set aside to reimburse Fugger, whereas the rest were funneled into the basilica construction fund. This accelerated the building of the palatial cathedral, fashioned out of marble, limestone, and brick, which continues to be a sight to behold today.

Albert of Brandenburg

Fugger

16th century woodcut depicting the sale of indulgences

When the German public caught on to the papal-approved scam, they were infuriated by the Church's distortion of God's word, as well as the Church's unabashed exploitation of the common people.

One of the first and most famous figures to raise a stink about this injustice was Martin Luther, a pious monk and a veteran in the fields of theology and philosophy. As a young monk, Luther was characterized as an highly devout and spiritual individual. He was stern by nature, but those around him were still taken aback by how severely self-critical he was. Luther found a second home in confessionals, where he inundated the priest on the other side with flood after flood of confessions every single day. It is said his intensity grew so overwhelming that even his spiritual director found him intolerable and thus gave him other work to keep the problematic monk preoccupied.

Luther

Luther became aware of the selling of indulgences in his lands sometime in 1517. While he had been critical regarding this practice before, the forcefulness of Tetzel's campaign made him see the need for a systematic treatment of this issue. To this purpose he wrote what is now known as the *95 Theses,* a document that expounded upon the errors of the indulgence practice and was originally meant for an academic disputation in Wittenberg. According to Melanchthon's biographical account, he also nailed them to the Church door in Wittenberg, "presumably to publicize the colloquium", though modern scholars now believe Luther's famous act of defiance was an apocryphal story.[1]

As Luther later recounted, he had attempted first to write to the Bishop Albrecht of Mainz but received no reply because the high Church official was also deeply involved in the matter:

> "... for he [Albert] was elected bishop of Mainz with the agreement that he was himself to buy the pallium [woolen mantle worn by archbishops as a symbol of office] at Rome. For three bishops of Mainz... had recently died, one shortly after the other, so that it was perhaps difficult for the diocese to buy the pallium so often

---

[1] Michael Mullet, p. 67

and in such quick succession, since it cost twenty-six or thirty thousand [gulden]...

Thus the bishop devised this scheme, hoping to pay the [banking firm of] the Fuggers (for they had advanced the money for the pallium) from the purse of the common man. And he sent this great fleecer of men's pockets [Tetzel] into the provinces...And in addition the pope had a finger in the pie as well, because one half was to go towards the building of St Peter's Church in Rome."[2]

At the time, however, Luther was not aware of who stood to profit directly from the money gained as a result of selling indulgences, basing his critique solely on the theological issue. Luther insisted that salvation and forgiveness for one's sins could not be bought with guldens but had to be obtained through genuine repentance and contrition, despite the propaganda to the contrary.

The 95 Theses also questioned the pope's legitimacy in a sentiment many shared but dared not vocalize: "Why does the pope, whose wealth today is greater than the wealth of the richest Crassus, build the basilica of St. Peter with the money of poor believers, rather than with his own money?"

Luther's work had the advantage of coming right around the time Gutenberg's printing press made the mass distribution of written works possible, and as a result, the "95 Theses" became a massive hit with people, thereby sowing the seeds of the Protestant Reformation. All across Europe, more of these "reformers," as they would be called, began to stand up to the Catholic Church. One of the most momentous turning points of the movement took place in England. There, the people, too, had begun to raise their guards against the Catholic Church. Everything seemed to come with a price – baptism, marriage, even burials. Those who wished for a place in Heaven would have to reserve an expensive plot on the Church-owned "holy" land, or so the Catholics preached. It was King Henry VIII who called for an official split from the Catholic Church. The monarch had wanted a divorce from his wife, Catherine of Aragon, due to her failure to conceive a male heir to the throne, a request that was rebuffed by the Catholics. Henry's eventual breakup with the Catholic Church led to the establishment of the Church of England. From that point on, Christendom was halved right down the middle – the Catholics and the Protestants, each side equally unyielding.

---

[2] Martin Luther, quoted in Michael Mullett, p. 68 - 69

Henry VIII

Another critical contributor to the Protestant Reformation was John Calvin, widely credited as Luther's successor, and for breeding the second generation of Protestantism. Born in Noyon, France, Calvin is mostly remembered for his cool and logical disposition, as well as his intrigue with God and theology at a young age. When Calvin became a law student at the University of Orléans, he opened his eyes to Protestantism. From there, this intrigue turned to a calculated obsession.

Calvin

In 1536, Calvin authored the "Institutes of the Christian Religion," a document that outlined his reformed views on Protestant beliefs. The ideas are best summed up with the acronym, "TULIP." To begin with, "T" represents "Total Depravity," meaning that humans are completely powerless, and cannot know God unless they are touched by God's own grace. Sinners are trapped in their sinful states, all exits bolted shut by God's fury. This idea is traced back to the biblical passages of Romans 3: 10–11, which reads, "As it is written, 'No one is righteous, no, not one; no one understands God, no one seeks for God."

"U" is for "Unconditional Election." This suggests that God has "predestined," or has already chosen a select group of the saved. Only He holds the key to salvation. No matter how high or low humans go to search for this key, those who have not been "chosen" will only be thwarted by dead ends.

"L" is for "Limited Atonement." This corresponds with the previous point, and illustrates that Christ has only saved Himself for a chosen group of people. While Christ may have been able to sacrifice Himself for all, He had only done so with the "elected" in mind. This rather grim revelation is supposedly supported by John 17:9, which states, "I am praying for them. I am not praying for the world, but for those whom you have given me, for they are yours."

"I" is for "Irresistible Grace." Sinners may initially reject God's love, but once they have been kissed by His spirit, they are incapable of resistance. As the almighty being that rules above all, God never fails when He chooses to redeem a soul on His list. Finally, "P" stands for "Perseverance of the Saints." This reaffirms that divine salvation is forever binding, as God would never allow the saved to slip through the cracks of His fingers.

The earliest Calvinist ideology revolved around *sola scriptura*, which meant that scripture held ultimate authority above everything in life. Calvinists believed that the Bible was a "direct revelation" from God, which clearly laid out the bylaws for His creation. The Holy Book, therefore, held divine authority.

Apart from the theory of "predestination," Calvinists believed – and still believe – in the sovereignty of God. The flawless and all-knowing God is said be in complete control over all that He has created. All that occurs in this world has already been carefully calibrated and planned out by the Lord. As God does not make mistakes, everything happens for a reason.

Many often misunderstand the meaning behind "predestination" and conclude that Calvinists do not believe in free will, as humans are supposedly powerless to change the courses of their own paths. Calvinists, however, do believe in a limited sense of free will – humans are perfectly capable of making their own choices, but only within the scope of "their nature." Calvinists claim that it is impossible to "choose salvation." While the sick might choose to undergo medication that may prolong their lives, dead men have no say in their unchangeable fates.

Though Calvinists might have been aware that God has already chosen his children, they know that humans have no way of procuring that classified list. It is then an individual's responsibility to make good choices and lead a life of wholesome Christian living. That being so, the individual is responsible for spreading the word to all they come across, and hope for the best.

Calvin dwelled in Geneva, Switzerland for a short spell until he was driven out by Catholic authorities in 1538. 3 years later, Geneva reopened their borders to Calvin, welcoming him back aboard as the head of the church. By then, he was one of the most respected spiritual and political leaders in all of Europe. Calvin's reign was peaceful and more or less uncontested, particularly in his final years. Apart from the various reforms he brought with him, Calvin housed "Marian exiles," or British Protestants fleeing from the Catholic monarchs in England. Genevan ministers were dispatched to all corners of Europe, including England, Netherlands, Scotland, and even the New World, bearing Calvin's rendition of God's Word. Nearing the top of Calvin's agenda were his intentions to reform France, his projects funded by the Church of Geneva. 100 of his best missionaries were stationed in his homeland, where they began to distribute pamphlets and other literature through an underground press network, away from the probing eyes of the authorities.

Geneva was established as the center of reformed Protestantism. As Calvinist pastors scattered across Europe, their various churches would soon develop names and communities of their own. The English Protestants came to be known as the "Puritans." In Scotland, they became the "Presbyterians." The Netherlands became home to the Dutch Reformed Church, the largest Christian denomination during the reformation era. Last, but not least, there were the French Protestants, who were later dubbed the "Huguenots."

The unconventional ideas of the flourishing Calvinist movement were especially controversial in a time when most of Europe was either Roman Catholic or Lutheran Protestant. Many dispelled Calvin's "radical" beliefs; the idea of having not an iota of control over their own fates or salvation, even through prayer or repentance, was unfathomable to the traditionalists. Still, a separate fraction knew of Calvin's legal background, and they were drawn to his logical dissection of Christianity's principles.

While many praised Calvin for his fresh perspective on an age-old religion, he was also knocked for leading a stringent, almost draconian reign. Creativity was stifled – all forms of art and music, apart from somber singing, was outlawed. Voices were silenced – at least 58 were executed, and another 76 banished for their non-Calvinist beliefs.

The tables were soon to turn.

Royals vs. Huguenots

"We have come to the determination to die, all of us, rather than abandon our God, and our religion..." – Jeane d'Albret, Queen of Navarre, to Catherine de Medici, Queen of France

In addition to the religious underpinnings of the Reformation that would bring about the conflicts between French Huguenots and French authorities, a number of important people played decisive roles in the events to come. First, there was Catherine de' Medici, the daughter of Lorenzo de' Medici, an Italian prince and the ruler of Florence, and his wife, Madeleine, the Countess of Boulogne. Catherine's birth was said to have delighted the giddy parents "as if it had been a boy." Unfortunately, the baby girl would lose both her parents within the span of a month; Madeleine had succumbed to a horrible fever brought about by the plague, while Lorenzo perished shortly thereafter from complications due to syphilis. Baby Catherine was first passed on to Lorenzo's mother, and her guardianship later entrusted to her aunt, Clarice.

Catherine

The de' Medici family tree boasted branches of royal and noble connections that tied them to the most prominent figures in all of European society, including Pope Leo X and Clement VII, both of whom were related to Lorenzo. The popes were said to have spotted a special glimmer of promise in young Catherine's eyes, and since she had been born only 2 years after Martin Luther's publication of the "95 Theses," and thus in the thick of the Protestant pandemonium, they seized the opportunity to mold her into the God-fearing Catholic she would one day become.

Pope Clement VII

In 1533, Pope Clement played matchmaker for 14-year-old Catherine and Prince Henry, the Duke of Orléans and the son of King Francis I of France, but the pair failed to make a connection. Just a year after the wedding, 15-year-old Henry entered a lascivious affair with a 35-year-old noblewoman, Diane de Poitiers, who had looked after – or perhaps, groomed him – throughout his tainted childhood. Diane was a certified stunner with a "skin of great whiteness," and she was unusually athletic, maintaining her youth through the religious intake of a golden elixir, a concoction of gold chloride and diethyl ether. The teenage Henry was hopelessly smitten.

Henry II of France

In 1536, Henry's brother, 18-year-old Francis III, collapsed after taking a drink of water following a tennis match. Lamentably, Francis died several days later, which prompted rumors that his water had been laced with poison, but either way, with Francis's death vacating a spot in the queue to the throne, Henry and Catherine were bumped up to the front. As anticipated, when King Francis passed on in 1547, Henry and Catherine were crowned King Henry II and Queen Catherine of France.

In the beginning of her reign, Catherine was no more than a titular puppet, and Henry made it no secret that he favored his mistress over his own wife. Henry and Diane were often seen entangled in each other's arms in public, even occasionally with Henry caressing Diane's breasts in full view of Catherine. While Diane was said to have secretly manned the operation behind the scenes, she allowed Henry to sleep with Catherine so they could produce valid heirs to the throne. Together, the husband and wife would have 10 children, and of the 10, 6 would survive to adulthood, among them sons Francis, Henry III, and Charles IX.

In an effort to unite against Protestantism in 1559, France and Spain decided to join forces, settling a decades-long territorial dispute with the Peace of Cateau-Cambrésis. This treaty was cemented with the matrimonial union between Prince Philip II of Spain and Catherine and Henry's daughter, Elisabeth.

Elisabeth

As fate would have it, their wedding bliss was promptly cut short when the French king was impaled in the eye by a lance during a jousting competition as part of a celebratory tournament in 1559. The tip of the lance pierced past his eyeball and into his brain, and Henry died a few days later of septicemia, which propelled their 15-year-old son, Francis II, to the throne. At 15, monarchs did not require a regent (a guardian who acted on their behalf), but given how green Francis II was, someone had to step up to the plate. Ultimately, regency was given to the uncles of his young wife Mary, Queen of Scots, meaning the monarchs of Scotland would at least temporarily control the French throne.

Francis II

It was around the beginning of Francis's rule that friction between the Catholic French and Huguenot Navarre royals truly began to whip up. Just a year into the Scotland-manipulated reign, Huguenot rebels sensed the vulnerability of the throne and pounced on the chance to eject Francis from his coveted seat. Luckily for him, the plot was discovered, and all 57 conspirators were sent to their immediate deaths.

When the sickly 16 year old king died from complications of an ear infection the year after, his 10-year-old brother, Charles IX, took his place. Deciding that it was high time for her to shine, Catherine eagerly accepted the available post of regency.

Charles IX

Another influential individual at this juncture was Jeanne d'Albret, the Catholic-raised cousin of the French royals, and the daughter of King Henry II of Navarre. At the age of 14, she, too, would be married off to William, the Duke of Cleves. Jeanne was strongly opposed to this decision, and heartily protested the marriage until her wedding day; in fact, the princess was said to have been so defiant that she had to be swept off her feet and carried to the altar, kicking and screaming. To Jeanne's relief, before the marriage could be consummated, the union was annulled with a papal stamp of approval, and in 1548, the 20-year-old Jeanne instead married the French royal Antoine de Bourbon, the Duke of Vendôme. The pair produced 2 children: Henry

IV and Catherine de Bourbon.

Jeanne

Antoine

Jeanne became the Queen of Navarre upon her father's death in 1555, and on Christmas Day five years later, she announced her conversion to Calvinism for the first time and declared it the official religion of her kingdom. This bold move made her the highest-ranking Protestant in all of France, and the Catholic Church just as quickly labeled her public enemy number one.

Jeanne displayed an unswerving discipline many never would have imagined from such a small, unassuming woman. She outlawed Catholicism, shut down one Catholic church after another, and banished nuns and priests by the dozens. She then ordered for a translation of the New Testament and distributed them among her subjects. At first, though it appeared as if her husband had also been converted, he did an about-face when he was offered dominion over Sardinia, an Italian island then owned by the Catholic King of Spain. But even then, Jeanne's shatterproof support remained with the Huguenots.

Apart from the dampening duo's religious differences, Jeanne and Antoine's amicable marriage began to crumble as they began to bicker over how they would raise their son, Henry. Antoine, under pressure from his own family, was said to have verbally and physically assaulted his wife repeatedly over this issue, often dangling the subject of divorce over her head. Antoine had even once flown into such a rage that he shoved her into a room and locked her up for days, but Jeanne would not falter from her new faith. She continued to promote Protestant teachings and hosted Huguenot ceremonies in her home.

Henry IV

Word of the quarreling couple's abusive marriage eventually spread, and when Catherine de' Medici learned of their marital issues, she reached out to Jeanne and pleaded with her to heed Antoine's words and reconvert to the Catholic faith. However, all attempts fell flat, and Jeanne's loyalty to the Huguenots would never be forgotten. Today, she is hailed as one of the first leading figures and religious reformers of the Huguenot movement.

Throughout the 1560s, Catherine, as regent, had chosen to keep her nose out of the ongoing

Protestant and Catholic wars, but the swelling population of Huguenots could no longer be ignored. By 1562, there were an estimated 2 million of the "heretics" in France. It was time to get her hands dirty.

In 1563, her dead husband's brother, Francis, the Duke of Guise, attempted to reclaim Orléans from the Huguenots but was fatally wounded by an assassin. A French admiral and avid Huguenot, Gaspard II de Coligny, along with another Protestant pastor, were accused of engineering the plot. The scoffing admiral swiftly asserted his innocence, but the embittered deceased's son, Henry I, who would soon be upgraded to the Duke of Guise, began to bear a jaundiced grudge against Coligny. Coupled with Queen Jeanne's protection of the Huguenots, who fought to seize control of France, the building tension between the Catholics and the Huguenots boiled over in 1562, spawning 8 civil wars in succession. These conflicts are now known collectively as the French Wars of Religion.

Admiral Gaspard II de Coligny

In 1570, the signing of the Peace of St. Germain halted the wars with a relatively brief interval of harmony and order. The terms of the treaty were made official through the arranged marriage of Catherine's daughter, Marguerite, and Prince Henry, Jeanne's son, which was scheduled for mid-August in 1572. As per the treaty, the Huguenots received dominion over several portions of southern France, which included Cognac, Montauban, La Rochelle, and La-Charité-sur-Loire. Another stipulation saw Admiral Coligny making his way back to his seat in royal court.

French Catholics were appalled by the decision to allow a Protestant back in court, and both the pope and King Philip II of Spain were among the most outspoken critics of the decision. Catherine knew full well of the controversy but bit the bullet anyway, hoping that Coligny would use his reinstated position to help quell the Huguenot outcries. Meanwhile, she would do her part with the Catholics.

The French public, both Protestant and Catholic, also took issue with the upcoming wedding. Devastated by unproductive harvests and a spike in food prices, they blamed the monarchs for the failing economy, and they were also aware the extravagant wedding would be funded with the taxpayers' money, which left a bad taste in their mouths. John Calvin's *Readings on the Prophet Daniel*, published 3 years prior to his death in 1561, did not help matters, as it firmly declared that all monarchs who disobeyed God "automatically abdicate[d] their worldly power." The Huguenots took this to heart, intensifying their resentment towards the Catholic monarch.

Catherine was reluctant to face the critics among her Catholic counterparts, but she soon began to regret her decision. Coligny had grown suspiciously close to King Charles IX, solidifying that bond as her son's personal adviser and most trusted confidante. It is believed that Catherine feared that her impressionable and naive 22-year-old son would fall victim to Coligny's Huguenot influence. Worse yet, she suspected that Charles was nothing more than a pawn for Coligny, who she believed was planning either another Huguenot uprising or a war with Spain.

On the 22nd of August, just 4 days after the royal wedding, Coligny was making his way home from the Louvre Palace when he was shot from a 2nd story window. As Coligny, who was only wounded, stumbled off for help, the perpetrator elbowed past the panicking mob, and vanished. Today, many are still unsure about who it was that contrived the assassination attempt, but the bulk of historians agree that it had been Catherine who approved it.

A contemporary engraving depicting the assassination attempt

An enraged King Charles set out to investigate the attempted murder to appease the Huguenots, but when he tried to pay his ailing friend a visit, Catherine quickly put a cork in it, severing all communication between the two. Once she had calmed Charles down, she managed to convince her son that the Huguenots were only a hair's away from mutiny, and she dragged Coligny's name through the mud, citing his alleged plans to seize control of the Catholic court. The king was livid. According to his brother's diary, Charles growled, "Kill the Admiral if you wish, but you must also kill all the Huguenots, so that no one is left alive to reproach me. Kill them all!"

Coligny's name was the first on the hit list. On August 24th, before dawn had even cracked, a vicious rabble, headlined by the surviving members of the Guise family, burst into Coligny's room. The dazed Coligny was pounded to a pulp before his attackers flung him out of the window, ending his agony. Catholic rebels all across Paris cried for Huguenot blood and took to the streets, rioting and joining in on a bloody killing spree immortalized today as the "St. Bartholomew's Day Massacre." King Charles issued a decree to cease the killings the following day, but the killings continued to spill into various provinces, tapering out only in October.

A painting depicting the massacre

The death toll from the massacre continues to be disputed, but historians estimate that 3,000 Huguenots died in Paris, and 70,000 in France as a whole. Bodies drifted down the Rhône River for months before the rotting corpses were finally cleared away. King Charles grew increasingly delirious day after day, haunted by nightmares and the cries of the dead in his ears. He once clung to his nurse, wailing, "What bloodshed, What murders! What evil counsel I have followed!" Never the same, Charles blamed his mother and himself until the day he died in May of 1574, at age 23.

A depiction of Catherine seeing the carnage outside of the Louvre

When Charles passed on, his brother and the fourth of Catherine's sons, Henry III, claimed his seat on the throne, and he would rule until his assassination in 1589. A demented Dominican friar, who had with him forged documents, was granted permission to the king's chambers. The friar requested for the guards to stand back, claiming the document to be of utmost confidentiality. When the guards tentatively obliged, the friar sprung forth and plunged a knife into the childless king's abdomen. Since Francis, the Duke of Anjou and the last of Catherine's sons, had died 5 years ago, all eyes fell upon the son of the famously Huguenot Queen Jeanne – King Henry IV of Navarre.

Henry III

In 1589, Henry became the first Bourbon king of the nation, and from then on, he was known as King Henry IV of France. He had born witness to the previous king's uncalculated decision-making skills – more precisely, an event in 1588 that contributed to his demise. The French Catholic public had grown discontented with the Catholic predecessor's seeming procrastination to establish solid laws that would protect France from Protestantism. Court officials were deemed lazy and incompetent. Others were convinced that the former Henry had been fraternizing with the Protestants, and was laying out the foundations for the Huguenot Henry of Navarre to succeed him. he people grew even more disconcerted by the presence of Swiss and French guards in Paris, placed there by Henry III. The uprising that ensued is now known as the "Day of the Barricades," which saw the disgraced king's ugly defeat in Paris. The humiliated Henry III vengefully ordered the deaths of several prominent Catholic members of the Guise family, including his own brother, a decision that would ultimately cost the king his life.

A depiction of the Duke of Guise during the Day of the Barricades

Now that he was in charge, King Henry IV hoped to bring an end to all the religious hostility. The only way to achieve this, he believed, would be to establish a society that ensured equality for all. Thus, on April 13, 1598, Henry signed the Edict of Nantes. The signing of this treaty ended the French Wars of Religion, which had taken the lives of over 3 million already. The document contained 92 articles that promised political and social equality for all of France, even the Huguenots. The Huguenots were now free to practice their religion, either in private, or publicly on Protestant-owned land, with no repercussions. As accepted members of society, they were granted equal education and health care, and were now allowed to inherit land and property. On May 2, amnesty was bestowed upon both sides of the war. Furthermore, the new king recompensed Protestant pastors, and provided financial support to 50 Huguenot towns.

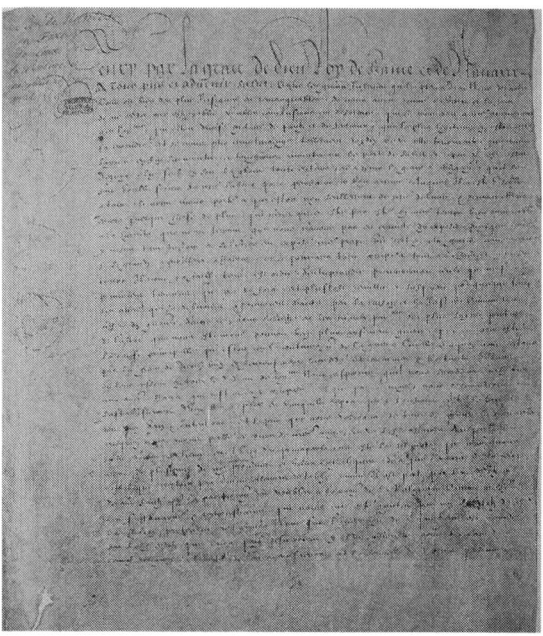

A copy of the Edict of Nantes

Despite Henry's attempt at peace and toleration, not everyone was bouncing with glee. Henry's marriage to Marguerite was an unhappy one, and both had already decided to part ways long before he became king. In his separation, he fell head over heels for his favorite mistress, the fair-haired and intoxicating Gabrielle d'Estrées. Besides being one of his most faithful cheerleaders, Gabrielle, a Catholic, always had a way with Henry. Her opinion was held in such high regard that she was able to persuade Henry to renounce his Huguenot faith and convert to Catholicism, which was then his only obstacle before the crown.

Legend has it that Henry was quickly swayed, apparently shrugging it off with the nonchalant remark, "Paris is well worth a mass." He soon shed his Huguenot leanings and became a reformed Catholic convert. Though this would win the respect of his new, predominantly Catholic subjects, the Huguenots were less than impressed with him for jumping ship. Many saw the king's edict as a coward's way out.

To Henry's dismay, Gabrielle suddenly died after a stillborn birth in 1599, ending their plans of marriage. The next year, the heartbroken Henry had his union with his first wife, Marguerite, officially annulled. Later that same year, he married yet another Catholic with a familiar name –

Marie de' Medici.

Marie

Throughout Henry's reign, he worked hard to maintain the new wave of peace and prosperity in his kingdom, and for a while, the people seemed to respond to him, with some even calling him "Good King Henry." Henry not only refilled the royal funds, he created reservoirs for future use. He modernized military training and equipment, and he ordered for the reconstruction of several governmental and art centers.

However, as much as he had hoped to curb the Catholic and Huguenot tensions, the animosity towards him lingered. The Catholics saw him as a secret Huguenot and greedy double-agent who had no real intentions of living the Catholic lifestyle. Huguenots, on the other hand, labeled him a treacherous traitor for his failure to stay true to his faith, as his mother, Queen Jeanne, had done.

As a result, Henry became the target for multiple assassination attempts, and the the third one would succeed. On May 14, 1610, the royal coach came skidding to a halt, and seemingly out of nowhere, a Catholic assassin lunged forth and drove a knife into the king's chest, killing him.

King Louis XIII

"To know how to dissimulate is the knowledge of kings." – Cardinal Richelieu, French clergyman and royal advisor

Louis XIII, the oldest son of King Henry IV and Marie de' Medici, was barely 9 years old at the time of his father's untimely death. In October of 1610, the child replaced the fallen monarch, and regency was granted to his mother, Marie. As a child, the pale and feeble Louis shivered and stuttered as he spoke. This led many to draw the conclusion that he was "taciturn," or in today's terms, autistic.

Louis XIII

In 1615, Marie arranged for the marriage of 14-year-old Louis and Anne of Austria, the teenager daughter of King Philip III of Spain. Their marriage was the final knot tied to honor the Treaty of Fontainebleau of 1611. The treaty guaranteed a 10-year alliance and mutual defense pact between France and Spain.

Louis and Anne would bear 2 children of their own: Louis XIV and Philippe I, the Duke of Orléans. The pair reportedly shared a cordial relationship with one another, but they lived in separation throughout most of their marriage. As a matter of fact, some speculate that Louis might have been homosexual or bisexual. Throughout his teenage years and well into adulthood, Louis was believed to have engaged in multiple romantic relationships with an array of court officials. Regardless of his much-publicized trysts with men, the king was nicknamed "Louis the Chaste" for never taking a female mistress.

By 1614, 13-year-old Louis had come of age. He fought for his right to lead France on his own accord, but Marie refused to let go of the reins and continued on as the "de facto ruler" for 3 more years. As the effective ruler, Queen Marie chose to retain most of the officials in her husband's court, barring Maximilien de Béthume, the Duke of Sully and a proud Huguenot. Even with the expulsion of de Béthume and the new restrictions on certain Huguenot practices, Marie chose to level tensions by maintaining her husband's edict to some degree.

Despite Marie's attempts to keep the peace, the Catholic and Huguenot rebels were less than amused by the meddling queen's antics. Henri, the Prince of Condé, was next in line to the throne after Gaston, Henry and Marie's second son, and the temptation of royal instability seized him, kindling the renegade inside of him. Henri proceeded to assemble a small band of mutineers and launched a coup, hoping to do away with the monarchs, but he received almost no support from the public and was quickly defeated by Marie's forces.

The flummoxed queen attempted to squash tensions by assembling the Estates General, a legislative and consultative body designed to tackle urgent national matters. Only, no issues with Huguenots and rebels were ever truly resolved, as the ineffective team dwelled on topics about France's relationship with the papacy instead of brainstorming legitimate solutions.

The next year, Marie made matters even more complicated when Concino Concini, an Italian politician and one of her husband's most trusted ministers, joined her entourage. Concini might have been a Catholic, but many tensed up at the thought of a foreigner in the country's cockpit. Marie's friendship with Concini triggered another rebellion led by Henri in 1616. This time, he had the full support of Huguenot leaders. Louis, who looked on from the sidelines, took this as a sign of the Huguenots' dishonorable nature; the event instilled in him the belief that none of the Huguenots could be trusted.

Concini

Marie and Henri eventually settled their differences with the Treaty of Loudun. The treaty's terms ensured that Henri would be given more power, and therefore deepened his involvement in the government. In exchange, Concini would be allowed to remain in court.

Even with Henri's new status in court, more grousing nobles turned up the flames under Queen Marie. Protests multiplied, calling for the dismissal of Concini, and Marie began to fear for Concini's life. Still, instead of backing down, the stubborn Marie had Henri cuffed and thrown behind bars, which only served to enlarge the already conspicuous targets on the backs of Marie and Concini.

In the meantime, 16-year-old Louis had struck up a close – and some say, romantic – relationship with the 38-year-old Charles d'Albert. Charles was the Grand Falconer of France, a high-ranking position within the royal household, responsible for tending to the king's birds, as well as organizing and administrating royal falcon hunts. The charming falconer began to criticize Marie's overbearing nature. He warned Louis that his mother had no intention of giving up her regency, and encouraged him to make his move before it was too late.

In late April of 1617, Louis led an aggressive uprising within the palace. Concini was slain by palace guards. His wife, Eleonora Galigai, was classified as a witch, and beheaded, her corpse torched 3 months later. Finally, Louis shunned his own mother from the kingdom and appointed Charles as the Duke of Luynes.

The palatial coup proved to accomplish nothing, as Charles proved to be every bit as spurned as Concini. He would later cancel the *paulette* tax. The judicial and other governmental departments were no longer required to cough up 1/60 of their annual earnings to the crown, which only provoked more discontent from the public.

The abnormally rapid passing of the royal torches left the people disoriented and aggravated, and it would not take long before they began to pick apart the new king's flaws as well. Just a year after Louis seized control of the throne, central Europe spiraled into a series of cutthroat military, political, and religious conflicts, now known as the "Thirty Years War." Louis found himself trapped in the middle. As the king of France, the longstanding French rivalry against the Austrian royals produced an incentive to ally with the Protestants. Alternatively, as a Catholic, he felt liable to show his support for the Holy Roman Emperor. The public wrote him off as an indecisive leader, one that could not stick to his guns.

Besides the cancellation of the *paulette*, the Huguenots' patience was dwindling. Louis had inherited quite a dilemma. When Henry IV converted to Catholicism, he promised Rome that he would restore Béarn and Navarre, 2 of the most prominent Huguenot strongholds, to the Catholic faith, and the ambitious Louis decided that the crown would fulfill that promise. As soon as he had been granted full supremacy of France, he called for the reinstatement of Catholic rights, along with the restoration of all Catholic property in Béarn. He hoped to smoothen the process by offering generous sums to the landowners, but the Huguenots would not budge.

Louis was irritated, but undaunted. He steered his sights towards Navarre, where he issued the same proclamations, effective immediately. By the end of 1619, he had succeeded in regaining control of both Béarn and Navarre. When Louis started on his journey back to Paris, however, the rebels slunk out of the shadows once more. Deciding that enough was enough, under the king's instruction, a swarm of royal soldiers descended into both regions. Huguenot leaders and rebels were rounded up, and the majority of them were forced into exile. The streets rang with the hollers and whoops of the king's Catholic supporters, who proceeded to loot and vandalize Huguenot cemeteries and places of worship.

The First Rebellion

"For the time will come when they will not tolerate sound doctrine, but according to their own desires, will multiply teachers for themselves because they have an itch to hear something new. They will turn away from hearing the truth and will turn aside to myths." –2 Timothy 4: 3-4

The Huguenots had grown frantic, terrorized by the fear that the rights and equal footing they had worked so hard to achieve was slowly slipping from their grasps. It was bad enough that Béarn had reverted to French Catholic territory, but the government of the once Huguenot city underwent a complete reshuffling, and after that it became a purely Catholic body. The tides were turning, and it seemed there was no time to left to squander, for they could be flushed out by the incoming wave of absolute Catholic suppression at any given moment.

On December 25, 1620, all available Huguenots were invited to a meeting by Henri, the Duke of Rohan, and his younger brother, Benjamin, the Duke of Soubise. The noble-born brothers have always been a formidable force. Their parents, René II of Rohan, the Prince of Leon, and Catherine de Parthenay, the heiress to an affluent Protestant family, were something of a power couple of their own. As a unit, the Rohan nobles were one of the most esteemed and widely-connected families across the entire continent.

Henri

TRES HAVT ET TRES ILLVSTRE PRINCE
BENIAMIN DE ROHAN DVC DE FRONTENAY
Mouvrat ~ *Baron de Soubize, et c.*

Benjamin

The brothers received a home-schooled education from their mother, Catherine, a brilliant mathematician and one of the most gifted scholars of her time. Many believe it was Catherine who whipped her sons into shape, preparing them for the greatness that lay in store for them. A high standard of education, Catherine believed, was only half of the equation, as resilience could only be achieved through the proper training of mind and body.

And so, when the Huguenot brothers reached their teenage years, they enlisted themselves in the military. Benjamin served an apprenticeship as a soldier under Maurice, the stadtholder of all Dutch Republic provinces and the future Prince of Orange. His older brother, Henri, seemed to have a natural penchant for the force. Henri excelled in almost every aspect of his military career, earning the respect and admiration of his various superiors. At age 16, Henri was said to have been blessed with a polished set of leadership skills, as well a flair for befriending characters from all backgrounds. He had even formed a close bond with King Henry IV, a notorious Catholic convert, and was said to have been one of the king's favorite associates. As Henri's military tours took him across Europe, he would also form an alliance with the English monarchs. The Huguenot was knighted in England, and he was later appointed godfather to the future King Charles I at the royal baptism.

Henri journeyed back to France in 1603, at the age of 24. Shortly after his arrival, King Henry IV invited him into the peerage by offering him the title of Duke. Henri, radiating with pride, gladly accepted. Previous plans that had been made of his marriage to Princess Catherine of Sweden fell through. That year, he married Marguerite de Béthume, the daughter of the future Duke of Sully. This was the very same Maximilien de Béthume who was removed from his post during Marie's Huguenot cleansing of the royal courts.

Henri proved to be an extraordinary addition to King Henry IV's military force, playing a significant role in leading the victorious campaign against the Duke of Bouillon in the early 17th century. Later, the brothers would also fight alongside Prince Maurice's troops to help subdue the Spanish armies. Henri's future looked brighter than ever, at least until the assassination of King Henry IV. When Queen Marie was granted control of France, she began a brutal campaign to stamp out the Huguenots. Under her reign, the influence of the so-called "Pious Party," a name designated to the rabidly anti-Protestant politicians, experienced a dramatic surge.

Henri was torn. The deeply patriotic Huguenot had always patted himself on the back for his unbiased loyalty to the crown, but Marie's anti-Huguenot campaign had careened out of control. This was followed by an even more suffocating reign enforced by King Louis XIII, which was certainly testing not only his faith but his character. Henri began by reducing himself to a shadow in government, keeping only a passive role as a form of subtle protest. But as the Huguenot morale worsened, Henri could sit on his hands no longer. Whether or not he had ever intended it, he would become the spearhead and face of the Huguenot resistance.

The forced conversions of Béarn and Navarre had been the final straw. The meeting organized by the Rohan brothers, which came to be known as the "General Assembly at La Rochelle," reached a consensus in no time: they vowed to snatch back what was rightfully theirs. To turn this desire into reality, they would assemble a group of the finest Huguenot soldiers, train them to a tee, and equip them with the most premium of weapons and equipment they could afford.

It was time to retire the monarchy, and erect a "state within a state." In this new community, the Huguenots would be independent from French rule, free to establish their own taxes, and free to build a proper army of their own. The Huguenots recalled John Calvin's endorsement in flouting any royal authority that sullied the word of God. After all, the Dutch, now a grand republic, had already once succeeded in doing so when they resisted and defeated their Spanish invaders. Towards the end of the meeting, captaincies and responsibilities were dispensed to those present at the meeting.

Word of the incoming Huguenot resistance managed to slither its way to France, and before long, King Louis XIII was alerted about the rumors. The flustered king scrambled into action, hastily piecing together his troops. In May of 1621, the first of Louis' troops posted themselves on the borders of the Huguenot city of Saumur, and the surrounding royal army laid siege to the undefended commune nestled in western France, cutting off all essentials, supplies, and aid to the city. Even though the Huguenots at Saumur had shown no inclinations of challenging Louis, the paranoid king decided not to take any chances, and he aimed to contain the madness before it spread. As expected, the unprepared city was an easy score.

Next, Louis directed his troops to the Huguenot stronghold of Saint-Jean-d'Angély, a small city tucked away in the southwestern region of country. Henri's less experienced brother, Benjamin, was entrusted with heading the defense. Benjamin had been stationed there in the hopes of weakening the royal forces before they could force their way into the main stronghold at La Rochelle. The younger Rohan put up a fight and stuck it out for 26 days before their inevitable surrender on June 24, 1621.

2 months later, the king and his forces marched on to the Huguenot stronghold of Montauban, but it was here that Louis XIII's luck began to wane. At 25,000, the size of his army was commendable, but the men were wobbling on their last legs. The men had grown disillusioned, malnourished, dehydrated, and generally exhausted from the nonstop fighting, and morale had sunk to an all-time low. The Huguenots of Montauban caught on to this and resisted the disintegrating royal forces. It took another 2 months before the French king finally admitted defeat and grudgingly retracted his troops.

Back home, Louis devoted his time to rebuilding and improving his forces. In June of the next year, the king was informed that one of his royal agents, who had been left in the Huguenot city of Négrepelisse, had been killed. And so, the king resumed his campaign with a fresh vengeance. He was keener than ever to teach the Huguenots a lesson, kick-starting one of his most merciless sieges yet. The new batch of royal troops poured into the city, looting, raping, and slaughtering the inhabitants and anything that lay in their wake, regardless of age, gender, or creed. Once they were finished, the riotous troops set the ruined city ablaze. These atrocities were carried out with the full support of Louis, who allegedly stated, "I command you to give no quarter to man, because they have irritated me, and shall be served as they have treated others." It was only after the city lay in smoking ruins that Louis realized that no such royal agent had existed, but what was done was done.

The guilt may have nibbled away inside of him, but outwardly, the king appeared remorseless. Just one month later, he proceeded to direct his troops to the vastly populated Huguenot city of Montpellier. Here, Louis and Henri tried their hand at a truce and began the negotiation of a peace treaty through a middleman, Marshal General Lesdiguières. On August 22, 1622, Louis and Henri signed the first draft.

In spite of Henri's encouragement, the hesitant Huguenots of Montpellier wanted no part of the deal and denied entry to the royal forces. For one, they could be in jeopardy of an unannounced attack by Henri, the Prince of Condé, who they believed had weaseled his way into the king's innermost circle. The Huguenot Henri tried to reason with them, but the residents of Montpellier insisted that they would only open their borders if King Louis agreed to a number of degrading conditions. Naturally, a disbelieving Louis refused and promptly ordered the immediate siege of the city, replacing Lesdiguières with Henri of Condé to head the mission.

Etienne d'Amérique, one of Henri's best agents, was elected to head the Huguenot defense for Montpellier. D'Amérique's extensive military background proved fruitful, as he managed to hinder the advancement of the royal troops for quite some time. Louis succeeded in overtaking Saint-Denis, the fortified base of Huguenot operations in Montpellier, but the Huguenots reclaimed their territory the very next day, exterminating 200 of the king's men in the process. On the same day, under the authority of Galonges, the head of the Montpellier garrison, 400 Huguenots emerged victorious over a royal army of 1,000.

The Huguenots' winning streak carried on. In early October, the Huguenots triumphantly countered 3 different attacks from the royal army. 300-400 of the 5,000 French soldiers were killed in the Huguenot retaliation, and thousands more were wounded. Supplies began to run low, and a great portion of the wounded royal soldiers petered out from infections and diseases. Louis finally hung his head and swallowed his defeat. Lesdiguières was once again tasked with creating the second draft of the treaty. On October 8, 1622, the Huguenot Henri arrived at Montpollier, bringing with him 4,000 men, outfitted with food, medicine, and other supplies. On the 19th of October, Henri and Louis shook hands and finalized the Treaty of Montpollier.

Louis agreed to reinstitute the Edict of Nantes and adhere to it once and for all. As for the Huguenots, they agreed to surrender their strongholds in Nîmes, Uzès, and Montpellier. The next day, King Louis returned to Montpellier, but this time, he came unarmed, and his forces slowly began to disassemble the Huguenot fortifications. The Citadel of Montpellier was built in its place and stocked with the Louis' most trusted underlings, which made it easier for the king to keep an eye on the town.

Take Two

"Secrecy is the first essential in affairs of state." – Cardinal Richelieu

For a while, it seemed as if the Treaty of Montpellier introduced a new chapter of peace and solidarity in France, but when Armand Jean du Plessis de Richelieu was appointed the king's Chief of Minister in 1624, it only spelled trouble for the Huguenots.

Cardinal Richelieu

Richelieu was born in Paris, the youngest son in a family of 7. The du Plessises were not noble men but fit snugly into the middle class. Richelieu's father was a soldier who was later appointed the Grand Provost of France, a powerful judge in the royal house who held jurisdiction over all its officers. His mother was the daughter of a notable law writer.

Tragedy struck when Richelieu was 5. His father had become a casualty during one of the battles of the religious civil war, news that sent his mother buckling to her knees. With the breadwinner deceased, debt quickly stacked up. It appeared that his father had not died in vain, as the crown swooped in and granted them royal aid, keeping them afloat. The monarch's assistance in their family's greatest crisis fostered Richelieu's growing respect and admiration for the crown.

Like Louis, Richelieu was a sickly and "delicate child," but he was by far the most academically gifted of all the du Plessis children. At age 9, he was admitted into the College de Navarre in Paris, where he explored the field of philosophy, and later, at 17, he took an interest in theology. With his studies behind him, he followed in his father's footsteps, and like many young men of his day, joined the army.

Apart from the royal aid granted to them by King Henry III, the du Plessises were elevated to a bishopric household, giving them authority over the diocese of Luçon, a Roman Catholic commune, as well as the Luçon Cathedral. Richelieu's mother had chosen to devote most of the financial aid to themselves, which quickly raised the local clergymen's ire. In an effort to placate the clergymen, Richelieu's mother offered to make her son, Alphonse, the bishop of Luçon. When Alphonse declined, choosing to becoming a monk instead, Richelieu's hand shot up. Not only was he a staunch Catholic, he was prepared to take this as another academic challenge.

In 1606, King Henry IV nominated 21-year-old Richelieu for the bishopric of Luçon, but Richelieu still required papal approval since he was still years under the age limit. The pope eventually awarded his blessings, and by the next year, Richelieu was a formally ordained bishop. He returned to Luçon in 1608, where he soon earned a reputation as a no-nonsense reformer and a champion of the reforms generated by the Council of Trent.

The Council of Trent was the core of the Counter-Reformation, the Catholic Church's response to the Protestant Reformation. It was an assembly of bishops who met together regularly between 1545 and 1563. Here, they identified Protestant heresies, outlined their beliefs for a better reaffirmation of their faith, and designed consequences for wayward Catholic leaders. Several changes were introduced, which included punishments and penalties for the crimes of simony, indulgences, and the housing of more than one diocese. Background checks for incoming priests became more meticulous, and all training on biblical knowledge and discipline more refined. Moreover, the council declared the Nicene Creed the official Catholic prayer, reinforced the doctrines of the Old and New Testaments, and established 7 sacraments. Catholic authorities applauded Richelieu's resolve to promote the new reforms and his admirable demonstration of leadership skills.

The young Richelieu later dipped his toe into the pool of politics. In 1614, he was invited to join the board of the Estates General, and swiftly became known as a vehement defender of Catholicism and the Trent reforms. Richelieu was also the first to argue in favor of tax exemption for the Catholic Church, and fought for the increase of bishopric influence in court. Catholic authorities began to see Richelieu as their equal, and even chose him to deliver the final speech during the last assembly.

After the scrapping of the Estates General, Richelieu began to involve himself with the crown. Louis XIII's wife, Anne of Austria herself, had taken notice of Richelieu and made him the Grand Almoner, or the director of religious affairs, of the royal household. He welcomed the new endeavor and continued to make strides, later scaling the ranks as a direct understudy of Marie de' Medici's partner in crime, Concini. Richelieu reached another milestone in 1616 when he was appointed the Secretary of State, granting him authority and management over foreign affairs. During this time, camaraderie evolved between Richelieu and Marie.

Richelieu's power would soon come crashing down. Following Concini's death and Marie's banishment in 1617, Richelieu was released from his post as Secretary of State. The next year, Louis, who singled Richelieu out for his very public friendship with Marie, ousted him to

Avignon. His ego was bruised, but Richelieu kept his head down and spent his exile churning out one work of literature after another. Perhaps he knew that it would only be a matter of time before power came back to him.

As he no doubt hoped, when Marie broke free from house arrest in 1619, a desperate Louis pleaded with Richelieu to return and talk some sense into the queen. He served as a medium for Louis and Marie, a task he handled with ease and flying colors. In a team effort with Louis' alleged lover, Charles, the Duke of Luynes, the pair managed to convince the squabbling mother and son to sign the Treaty of Angoulême. Through the terms of the treaty, the pair vowed to set aside their differences. What was more, Marie would be pardoned and granted her full freedom if she agreed to respect her son's authority.

The Duke of Luynes died suddenly from a fever 2 years later, and it was then that Richelieu began to inch closer to Louis. He gradually won the king's trust, and in 1622, he was nominated as a candidate for cardinal, which was later approved by the pope that same year. When the Huguenot Rebellions began, Louis repeatedly turned to Richelieu for counsel, and regarded his advice with the highest esteem. It seemed that only Richelieu was on the king's wavelength; the cardinal once wrote, "So long as the Protestants of France are a state within a state, the King cannot be master of his realm or achieve great things abroad."

In April of 1624, Richelieu's presence was requested at the king's royal council of ministers once more. As Richelieu settled into the familiar seat of power, the observant and shrewd cardinal sniffed out a rat. He published articles and pamphlets outing the Chief Minister and Superintendent of Finances, Charles de La Vieuville. When these rumors of Vieuville's corruption were validated, the discredited official escaped the gallows and fled to the Netherlands for refuge. Richelieu dusted off the vacant seat of Chief Minister and remained the nominal president for the council for years, until he was officially granted the title in 1629.

Often hailed as one of the greatest French politicians of all time, Richelieu was an ardent monarchist who aimed to consolidate his beloved nation of France in a unified and centralized government. In 1624, there remained 8 Huguenot circles, each piloted by their own commander-in-chief. This was essentially a republic inside a monarchy, otherwise known as the crown's nightmare-come-true. The Huguenots even had the gall to create their own general and provincial assemblies, which Richelieu lambasted as a "political monstrosity."

As a loyal Catholic, Richelieu had never made it a point to suppress his disdain for the Huguenots, but he knew that in order to achieve the harmonious, centralized society he so thirsted for, he would have to treat the Protestants with toleration and civil decency. Though the sight of the heretic Huguenots worshiping in public made his skin crawl, he respected the edict and kept his lips sealed. However, when the Huguenots decided to wreak havoc on the crown, Richelieu decided he would tolerate them no more.

Not long after the construction of the Citadel of Montpellier, Louis began to backpedal from the terms of the treaty. Louis had agreed to dismantle the royal fortifications in certain Huguenot strongholds, but instead, under the king's instruction, a marquis was tasked with strengthening the crown-owned Fort Louis in La Rochelle. To make matters worse, Louis was in the process of assembling a naval fleet in the nearby Blavet River, by the northwestern region of Brittany. Benjamin summoned the equally perplexed Huguenot leaders of La Rochelle. The suspicious circumstances provoked a quick conclusion. The king's push for peace was anything but sincere – once the Huguenots lowered their guards, the royal fleets would block off the ports to the city, making it easy to invade.

In early 1625, a manifesto penned by Benjamin began to circulate, warning the Huguenots about the pending attack and calling for a second insurrection. Benjamin sprang into action. First, he led his troops to the Isle of Ré, near La Rochelle, and took control of the island. There, he managed to amass a humble fleet of 12 small, but sturdy boats, and a crew of 100 sailors and armed soldiers. Later that January, Benjamin sailed towards Blavet, where his fleet fenced in the 6 stupefied vessels of the French Navy. The handsome, glinting ships may have been decked out with fresh paint and dozens of bronze cannons, but their stockpile of manpower and ammunition were nowhere near enough to ward off their attackers. The navy raised a white flag and surrendered several of their ships. The Huguenots' prized booty of the day was the *La Vierge*, a 500-ton beast of a vessel armed with 80 cannons.

Back at the harbor, the rattled Duke of Vendôme rolled out the boom, a barrier in the form of a strong, floating chain, and reeled it from one side of the harbor to the other. The Huguenot fleet refused to back down, and after a relentless 2-week effort, the chain finally snapped. At this point, Benjamin appeared a promising victor, commanding a splendid fleet of 70 ships.

For 3 weeks, the Huguenots fought to take control of the fort at Brittany, but they ultimately failed to secure the base. Defeated but undeterred, Benjamin retreated to the island to recuperate and went back to work. This time, he took 15 ships with him to the Isle of d'Oléron, and succeeded in occupying the new island. Benjamin's brave ventures did not go unnoticed, and soon, many began to look up to him as the new unofficial leader of the Huguenots. He, too, had dubbed himself the "Admiral of the Protestant Church." With the French Navy virtually extinguished, the Huguenot victory seemed imminent.

Not surprisingly, the French king flew into a rage when he heard of his navy's embarrassing failure to restrain the Huguenots. He promptly sought out the guidance of Charles, the Duke of Guise, and together, the pair formed a plan to retrieve the islands. They appealed to their allies for aid and were able to secure 20 Dutch warships. Richelieu even managed to organize a tit-for-tat with the Parliament representatives from England. Pursuant to the terms of the agreement, England would loan France 8 English vessels, and in return, France vowed to support the English forces in their campaign against Spain. The latter exchange would trigger a controversy of its own, as this meant that the Anglican king would be contributing to the destruction of a fellow Protestant force, but after much goading from Parliament, the reluctant King Charles I of England agreed.

Charles I of England

Thanks to all these moves, the French Navy resurfaced, stronger than ever, and set sail for the islands. The Huguenot fleets were ready to receive them, but they had clearly underestimated the size of the retaliating forces. Nevertheless, the Catholic and Huguenot fleets faced off. In July, a hail of cannons and artillery fire from Benjamin's fleet rained upon a Dutch ship, blowing up the vessel and all 300 soldiers inside of it. The month after, the Huguenots of La Rochelle linked forces with Benjamin in a collaborative effort to sink the French Navy. In September, all efforts of resistance were rendered futile when the French royalists conquered what was left of the

Huguenot vessels in Les Sables d'Olonne. 3,000 royal soldiers paraded into the islands, and the crown assumed control once again.

When things eventually simmered down, both parties began a lengthy session of peace negotiations. In February of 1626, Louis and the Huguenots shook hands once more, finalizing the Treaty of Paris. Religious freedom for all was both reaffirmed and restored, guaranteed only if those at La Rochelle agreed to disband their fleet and retire one of their forts in Tasdon. As for Benjamin, the disheartened Huguenot disappeared to England.

The Final Stand

"I die a Christian according to the profession of the Church of England, as I found it left me by my father...I have good cause and I have a gracious God. I will say no more." – King Charles I of England

The nation of England was deeply offended by their king's decision to provide support for the Catholic French. A brooding King Charles I was tormented by his own decision, his gut twisting with regret.

His countrymen's aversion towards his new bride, Henrietta Maria of France, only sprinkled more salt into the wound. Henrietta Maria was the youngest daughter of King Henry IV and Queen Marie, a plain-faced princess with a passion for the arts. In mid-June of 1625, shortly before her 16th birthday, Henrietta was wedded off to 25-year-old Charles. In that same ceremony, Charles was officially crowned the new king of England.

Henrietta Maria of France

Not unlike most arranged marriages, the couple got off to a rocky start. Henrietta did not speak a lick of English, and she would never fully grasp the language, let alone attempt to assimilate or educate herself on traditional English customs. She was "unapologetically" Catholic during a time when admitting to the faith in England could mean a death sentence. The young princess also had an insatiable appetite for luxury, demonstrated by the chests of jewels, diamonds, embroidered gowns in satin and velvet, and other valuables she had brought from home.

Apart from her heretical faith and hedonistic tendencies, those who despised Henrietta colored her as an "intrinsically apolitical, undereducated, and frivolous" queen. Many began to speculate that Henrietta was either a plant or a French spy, one conspiring to hand the key to England's kingdom over to France. Even as Charles and Henrietta eventually began to click and grew closer over time, the public still questioned the new king's support of the Protestant Church of England and did not appreciate his blossoming alliance with his Catholic wife.

Bearing this in mind, Charles was determined to refresh his public image. In 1626, shortly after the signing of the Treaty of Paris, rumors of a secret alliance between France and Spain began to make its rounds. This angered the already troubled Charles, for he now believed that the French, who had promised their support in England's ongoing war against Spain, had gone back on their word. When Charles' officials informed him that France was rebuilding their naval forces, the king was convinced France and Spain were plotting against him.

England's thorny relationship with Spain had taken a turn for the worse 3 years prior. Before Henrietta, Charles had been obsessed with Princess Maria Anna, the sister of the Spanish King Philip IV. His infatuation with the breathtaking princess was so strong that he felt compelled to travel to Spain. There, he approached Philip to request his sister's hand in marriage. In response, Philip commanded Charles to convert to Catholicism and remain in Spain for a year as a symbol of the future English-Spanish alliance, but Charles would not have it. He turned him down, and soon after, he declared war on Spain. Charles had hoped that he would have better luck with an alliance with the French, but it seemed as if history was only repeating itself.

Philip IV

In June of 1626, Walter Montagu, an English secret agent, was sent to La Rochelle, where he called for a meeting with the Rohan brothers and other Huguenot leaders. The attendants drew up plans for a third rebellion, the greatest one of them all. Montagu gave the Huguenots his word – this time around, they would have the full backing of the English troops.

A year later, the English royal George Villiers, the 1st Duke of Buckingham, parked his fleet of

100 ships and 7,000 men on the shore of the Isle de Ré. Villiers' high spirits were dulled when he realized that in the time that had passed, many of the Huguenots now had cold feet, and those at the island were no different.

Villiers

Be that as it may, Villiers was here on a mission, and he intended to see it through. He gathered his forces and forged on to seize the monarch-owned fortress of Saint-Martin, a move that kicked off the Anglo-Dutch War of 1627. The 1,200 foot soldiers and 200 horsemen stationed in Saint-Martin sounded the alarm bells and hastened into position, resisting the barrage of English troops. The back-and-forth dragged on for weeks, eating away at the supplies and ammunition of the English. Backups consisting of Scottish and Irish troops were delayed, and many of the vessels were gobbled up by unanticipated storms.

Conversely, the French troops, given a home court advantage, found it much easier to restock on supplies. Richelieu knew that the capture of Saint-Martin could very well mean the end of the French monarchy, so he exerted himself and managed to scrape together 20,000 more soldiers for the defense. Next, he offered an attractive reward to anyone in the kingdom who could first succeed in transporting 50 barrels of biscuits, corn, and flour to the French troops.

On the 5th of November, Villiers and his troops staggered back to Saint-Martin and attempted a final shot at redemption, but the withering army could only scratch up the walls of the fortress before they were driven out by the French troops. They bolted to the northern corner of the island, staving off the French troops along the way. By the end of the ordeal, Villiers had lost almost 5,000 of his 7,000 men. 3 days later, the remaining English troops filed into their battered vessels and sailed back home to England.

While Villiers and his men attempted to seize Saint-Martin, the crown's emergency plans had been set in motion. Back in August of 1627, a royal force consisting of 7,000 soldiers, 600 stallions, and 24 grand cannons were directed to the Huguenot center of La Rochelle. There, the preemptive troops began to secure and amp up the defense of the Fort Louis and Bongraine fortifications.

Now that the Isle of Ré had been recovered, Richelieu pinned his focus on La Rochelle. Richelieu, the second-in-command to Louis, was given complete authority over the French troops. His plan to barricade the enormous city's ports seemed almost absurd, but Richelieu ignored the naysayers and unfurled the blueprints. The new barricade was inspired by the causeway (a raised track above the water) Alexander the Great had built during the Siege of Tyre. Construction began in October, and by the next month, the French troops had erected a whopping "siege line" stretching 7 miles long, complete with 11 improved and 18 new fortifications.

The causeway was completed in January of 1628, and at last, Richelieu unveiled his floating barrier of 56 tethered and fully-armed royal vessels around the border of La Rochelle. In March of that year, the Huguenot leaders in the city gathered and elected Jean Guiton as mayor. Guiton wasted no time and quickly designed a defense strategy.

2 months later, additional English reinforcements arrived, headed by Lord Denbigh, but a week later, when Denbigh learned that a Spanish naval force was on its way to shore up the defense for the French troops, the English packed up and left abruptly. In late September, a larger English fleet made an attempt to deliver food, supplies, and more ammunition for the Huguenots, but they were deflected by French troops at the border. They were left with no choice but to make a dramatic U-turn and sail back to where they came from, without ever once setting foot on shore.

The Huguenots at La Rochelle resisted for several months, but aid from the English slowly began to fizzle out. Gradually, the French, bolstered by their Dutch and Spanish comrades, trounced the Huguenot armies. By the end of the 14th month, the population in La Rochelle had plummeted from 27,000 to 5,000. Henri of Rohan struggled to push the rebellion back on its tracks for some time, but the Huguenots were defeated in the sieges of Privas and Alès. Submission was inescapable, and in June of 1629, the Huguenots finally surrendered.

A depiction of the Siege of La Rochelle

3 months later, on the 27th of September, King Louis XIII and the Huguenot leaders reached a truce in the Treaty of Alès, otherwise known as the "Edict of Alès," or the "Edict of Grace." The document guaranteed freedom of worship to all the Huguenots of France, under the condition that they relinquish all political and territorial rights. No longer were they allowed to own French land or property, and they were now banned from participating in public office. In addition, all Huguenot fortresses were to be destroyed, and dominion over previously Huguenot cities was returned to the crown.

As Louis and Richelieu had always hoped, France was once again an absolute monarchy with sovereignty across the country. Moreover, these new changes drained the power of the Huguenot movement, leaving them utterly defenseless against the next wave of oppression. In 1685, King Louis XIV, the son of Louis XIII and Anne, nullified the Edict of Nantes, and with that, the legendary Sun King unleashed another era of Huguenot persecution. Consequently, 200,000 Huguenots would skedaddle to Protestant-friendly countries such as Prussia, Britain, and the Netherlands.

Louis XIV

Online Resources

Other books about Catholic history by Charles River Editors

Other books about French history by Charles River Editors

Other books about the Huguenots on Amazon

Bibliography

Authors, Huguenot Society. "Huguenot History." *The Huguenot Society of Great Britain and Ireland*. The Huguenot Society of Great Britain & Ireland, 2013. Web. 20 Feb. 2017. <http://www.huguenotsociety.org.uk/history.html>.

Tempest, Stephen. "What were the Huguenot rebellions?" *Quora*. Quora, Inc., 24 May 2016. Web. 20 Feb. 2017. <https://www.quora.com/What-were-the-Huguenot-rebellions-Can-someone-explain-them-as-if-I-were-a-little-kid-I-need-an-answer-soon-please-I-cannot-really-understand-them>.

Editors, Got Questions. "What is Reformed Theology?" *Got Questions.Org*. Got Questions Ministries, 2011. Web. 20 Feb. 2017. <https://www.gotquestions.org/reformed-theology.html>.

Editors, History Channel. "THE REFORMATION." *History Channel*. A&E Television Networks, LLC, 2014. Web. 20 Feb. 2017. <http://www.history.com/topics/reformation>.

Editors, Reference. "What caused the Protestant Reformation?" *Reference*. IAC Publishing, LLC, 2012. Web. 20 Feb. 2017. <https://www.reference.com/history/caused-protestant-reformation-75b4667fde8fa690#>.

Petersen, Randy. "Selling Forgiveness: How Money Sparked the Protestant Reformation." *Christianity Today*. Christianity Today Ministry, 1987. Web. 20 Feb. 2017. <http://www.christianitytoday.com/history/issues/issue-14/selling-forgiveness-how-money-sparked-protestant.html>.

Webley, Kayla. "Top 10 Controversial Popes." *Time*. Time, Inc., 14 Apr. 2010. Web. 20 Feb. 2017. <http://content.time.com/time/specials/packages/article/0,28804,1981842_1981844_1981624,00.html>.

Löffler, Klemens. "Pope Leo X." *The Catholic Encyclopedia*. Robert Appleton Company, 1910. Web. 20 Feb. 2017. <http://www.newadvent.org/cathen/09162a.htm>.

Editors, Medievalists.Net. "Naughty Nuns and Promiscuous Monks: Monastic Sexual Misconduct in Late Medieval England." *Medievalists.Net*. WordPress, 20 Sept. 2012. Web. 20 Feb. 2017. <http://www.medievalists.net/2012/09/naughty-nuns-and-promiscuous-monks-monastic-sexual-misconduct-in-late-medieval-england/>.

O'Malia, Miles Joseph. "Albert of Brandenburg." *The Catholic Encylopedia*. Robert Appleton Company, 1907. Web. 20 Feb. 2017. <http://www.newadvent.org/cathen/01262a.htm>.

Steinmetz, Greg. "Goldenballs." *The Economist*. The Economist Newspaper, Ltd., 30 July 2015. Web. 20 Feb. 2017. <http://www.economist.com/news/books-and-arts/21660074-not-nothing-was-jacob-fugger-known-jacob-rich-goldenballs>.

Authors, WikiSpaces. "The Engineering Behind Saint Peter's Basilica." *WikiSpaces*. Tangient, LLC, 16 Sept. 2013. Web. 20 Feb. 2017. <https://engineeringrome.wikispaces.com/The Engineering Behind Saint Peter%27s Basilica>.

Editors, Biography.Com. "John Calvin Biography." *Biography*. A&E Television Networks, LLC, 7 Oct. 2016. Web. 20 Feb. 2017. <http://www.biography.com/people/john-calvin-9235788#synopsis>.

Trueman, C. N. "The Reformation." *The History Learning Site*. The History Learning Site, Ltd., 16 Aug. 2016. Web. 20 Feb. 2017. <http://www.historylearningsite.co.uk/tudor-england/the-reformation/>.

Geisler , Norman L., and Ralph E. MacKenzie. "What Is Sola Scriptura?" *Christian Research Institute*. Christian Research Institute , 2011. Web. 20 Feb. 2017. <http://www.equip.org/article/what-is-sola-scriptura/>.

Smith, Jeff. "2 Beliefs That Set the Dutch Reform Church Apart From Other Christians." *Newsmax*. Newsmax Media, Inc., 2 Apr. 2015. Web. 20 Feb. 2017. <http://www.newsmax.com/FastFeatures/dutch-reformed-church-christians-beliefs/2015/04/02/id/636090/>.

Editors, Encyclopedia.Com. "HUGUENOTS." *Encyclopedia.Com*. The Gale Group, Inc., 2004. Web. 20 Feb. 2017. <http://www.encyclopedia.com/philosophy-and-religion/christianity/protestant-denominations/huguenots>.

Authors, Visit Holland. "Huguenot in Amsterdam." *Visit Holland*. Netherlands Board of Tourism, 2008. Web. 20 Feb. 2017. <http://www.visitholland.nl/index.php/history/98-huguenot-in-amsterdam>.

Slick, Matthew J. "The Five Points of Calvinism." *The Calvinist Corner*. Matthew J. Slick, 2012. Web. 20 Feb. 2017. <https://www.calvinistcorner.com/tulip.htm>.

Trueman, C. N. "Catherine De Medici." *The History Learning Site*. The History Learning Site, Ltd., 27 May 2015. Web. 20 Feb. 2017. <http://www.historylearningsite.co.uk/france-in-the-sixteenth-century/french-wars-of-religion/catherine-de-medici/>.

Authors, Encyclopedia of World Biographies. "Catherine de' Medici Biography." *Encyclopedia of World Biographies*. Advameg, Inc., 16 Mar. 2007. Web. 20

Feb. 2017. <http://www.notablebiographies.com/Ma-Mo/Medici-Catherine-de.html>.

Samuel, Henry. "French king's mistress poisoned by gold elixir." *The Telegraph*. Telegraph Media Group, Ltd., 22 Dec. 2009. Web. 21 Feb. 2017. <http://www.telegraph.co.uk/news/worldnews/europe/france/6865939/French-kings-mistress-poisoned-by-gold-elixir.html>.

Guilliotine, Madame. "Diane de Poitiers – cougar, gold drinker, fashionista." *Madame Guilliotine*. WordPress, 26 Mar. 2011. Web. 21 Feb. 2017. <http://madameguillotine.org.uk/2011/03/26/diane-de-poitiers-cougar-gold-drinker-fashionista/>.

Editors, History Channel. "Saint Bartholomew's Day Massacre." *History Channel*. A&E Television Networks, LLC, 24 Aug. 2010. Web. 21 Feb. 2017. <http://www.history.com/this-day-in-history/saint-bartholomews-day-massacre>.

Lewis, Jone Johnson. "Jeanne d'Albret - Jeanne of Navarre." *About Education*. About, Inc., 5 Sept. 2015. Web. 21 Feb. 2017. <http://womenshistory.about.com/od/protestant/a/jeanne_dalbret.htm>.

Editors, Encyclopedia.Com. "Henry IV (France) (1553–1610; Ruled 1589–1610)." *Encyclopedia.Com*. The Gale Group, Inc., 2004. Web. 21 Feb. 2017. <http://www.encyclopedia.com/people/history/french-history-biographies/henry-iv-france>.

Cavendish, Richard. "The Edict of Nantes." *History Today*. History Today, Ltd., 4 Apr. 1998. Web. 21 Feb. 2017. <http://www.historytoday.com/richard-cavendish/edict-nantes>.

Editors, Reference. "What did the Edict of Nantes do?" *Reference*. IAC Publishing, LLC, 2011. Web. 21 Feb. 2017. <https://www.reference.com/history/did-edict-nantes-acc0b04d2495f33c>.

Editors, Biography.Com. "Louis XIII Biography." *Biography*. A&E Television Networks, LLC, 12 Feb. 2015. Web. 21 Feb. 2017. <http://www.biography.com/people/louis-xiii-9386868>.

Editors, The Famous People. "Louis XIII of France Biography." *The Famous People*. The Famous People, Ltd., 2009. Web. 21 Feb. 2017. <http://www.thefamouspeople.com/profiles/louis-xiii-of-france-6768.php>.

Editors, Encyclopedia Britannica. "Concino Concini, marquis d'Ancre." *Encyclopedia Britannica*. Encyclopedia Britannica, Inc., 20 July 1998. Web. 21 Feb. 2017. <https://global.britannica.com/biography/Concino-Concini-Marquis-dAncre>.

Authors, Executed Today. "1617: Eleonora Galigai, Marie de' Medici favorite." *Executed Today*. WordPress, 8 July 2016. Web. 22 Feb. 2017. <http://www.executedtoday.com/tag/concino-concini/>.

Trueman, C. N. "Louis XIII and religion." *The History Learning Site*. The History Learning Site, Ltd., 17 Mar. 2015. Web. 22 Feb. 2017. <http://www.historylearningsite.co.uk/france-in-the-seventeenth-century/louis-xiii-and-religion/>.

Editors, History Channel. "THIRTY YEARS' WAR." *History Channel*. A&E Television Networks, LLC, 2013. Web. 22 Feb. 2017. <http://www.history.com/topics/thirty-years-war>.

Chery, Fritz. "Rebellion." *Bible Reasons*. Bible Reasons, Ltd., 13 July 2015. Web. 22 Feb. 2017. <http://biblereasons.com/rebellion/>.

Authors, Virtual Museum of Protestantism. "Henri de Rohan (1574-1638)." *Virtual Museum of Protestantism*. Virtual Museum of Protestantism, 2000. Web. 22 Feb. 2017. <http://www.museeprotestant.org/en/notice/henri-de-rohan-1574-1638-2/>.

Editors, Wiki Visually. "Benjamin, Duke of Soubise." *Wiki Visually*. Wikimedia Foundation, Inc., 27 July 2016. Web. 22 Feb. 2017. <http://wikivisually.com/wiki/Benjamin,_Duke_of_Soubise>.

Trueman, C. N. "Cardinal Richelieu and the Huguenots." *The History Learning Site*. The History Learning Site, Ltd., 20 Oct. 2016. Web. 22 Feb. 2017. <http://www.historylearningsite.co.uk/france-in-the-seventeenth-century/cardinal-richelieu-and-the-huguenots/>.

Editors, Wiki Visually. "Siege of Nègrepelisse." *Wiki Visually*. Wikimedia Foundation, Inc., 16 Oct. 2016. Web. 22 Feb. 2017. <http://www.wikivisually.com/wiki/Siege_of_N%C3%A8grepelisse>.

Goyau, Georges. "Diocese of Montauban." *The Catholic Encylopedia*. Robert Appleton Company, 1911. Web. 22 Feb. 2017. <http://www.newadvent.org/cathen/10524a.htm>.

Editors, Revolvy. " Citadel of Montpellier ." *Revolvy*. Revolvy, LLC, 2012. Web. 22 Feb. 2017. <https://www.revolvy.com/topic/Citadel%20of%20Montpellier&item_type=topic>.

Editors, New World Encyclopedia. "Cardinal Richelieu." *New World Encylopedia*. MediaWiki, 10 Jan. 2017. Web. 22 Feb. 2017. <http://www.newworldencyclopedia.org/entry/Cardinal_Richelieu>.

Editors, Reference. "What were the results of the Council of Trent?" *Reference*. IAC

Publishing, LLC, 2015. Web. 22 Feb. 2017. <https://www.reference.com/world-view/were-results-council-trent-5151256673f19291>.

Rasmussen, Martha. "The Tale of Trent: A Council and and Its Legacy." *Ignatius Insight*. Ignatius Press, 2006. Web. 23 Feb. 2017. <http://www.ignatiusinsight.com/features2006/mrasmussen_trent_feb06.asp>.

Authors, Erenow. "'That Idiot'." *Erenow*. Erenow, LLC, 2015. Web. 23 Feb. 2017. <http://erenow.com/biographies/the-bourbon-kings-of-france/4.html>.

Editors, Wiki Visually. "Battle of Blavet." *Wiki Visually*. Wikimedia Foundation, Inc., 14 Oct. 2016. Web. 23 Feb. 2017. <http://wikivisually.com/wiki/Battle_of_Blavet>.

Simkin, John. "King Charles I." *Spartacus Educational*. Spartacus Educational Publishers, Ltd., Nov. 2016. Web. 23 Feb. 2017. <http://spartacus-educational.com/STUcharles1.htm>.

Editors, Camelot International. "MARY, QUEEN OF SCOTS." *Camelot International - The Tower of London*. Knight International Bulgarian Property Specialist, 2007. Web. 23 Feb. 2017. <http://www.camelotintl.com/tower_site/speeches/index.html>.

Editors, Revolvy. " Anglo-French War (1627–1629) ." *Revolvy*. Revolvy, LLC, 2012. Web. 23 Feb. 2017. <https://www.revolvy.com/main/index.php?s=Anglo-French%20War%20(1627%E2%80%931629)>.

Editors, Revolvy. " Henrietta Maria." *Revolvy*. Revolvy, LLC, 2015. Web. 23 Feb. 2017. <https://www.revolvy.com/topic/Henrietta%20Maria&item_type=topic>.

Plancon, Michel. "Saint-Martin-de-Ré." *Fortified Places*. WordPress, 1999. Web. 23 Feb. 2017. <http://www.fortified-places.com/saintmartin.html>.

Editors, Weapons and Warfare. "Siege of La Rochelle." *Weapons and Warfare*. WordPress, 30 Aug. 2015. Web. 23 Feb. 2017. <https://weaponsandwarfare.com/2015/08/30/siege-of-la-rochelle/>.

Cottret, Bernard. *Calvin: A Biography*. N.p.: Wm. B. Eerdmans Publishing Company, 2000. Print.

Major, David C., and John S. Major. *A Huguenot on the Hackensack: David Demarest and His Legacy*. N.p.: Fairleigh Dickinson U Press, 2007. Print.

Knecht, R. J. *Catherine de'Medici*. 1st ed. N.p.: Routledge, 1997. Print.

Bly, Robert W. *The Words You Should Know to Sound Smart: 1200 Essential Words Every Sophisticated Person Should Be Able to Use*. N.p.: Adams Media, 2009. Print.

Cooper, J. P. *The New Cambridge Modern History, Vol. 4: The Decline of Spain and the Thirty Years War 1609-48/59* . N.p.: Cambridge U Press, 1970. Print.

Crowe, Eyre Evans. *The History of France*. Vol. 3. N.p.: Facsimile Publisher, 2013. Print.

Jackson, Richard. *(Re)Constructing Cultures of Violence and Peace*. N.p.: Rodopi , 2004. Print. At the Interface/Probing the Boundaries.

Richey, Tom. "Calvinism (Introduction to John Calvin's Reformed Theology)." *Tom Richey Channel*. YouTube. 13 Oct. 2014. *YouTube*. Web. 24 Feb. 2017. <https://www.youtube.com/watch?v=KZARuVXiH8k>.

Richey, Tom. "French Wars of Religion." *Tom Richey Channel*. YouTube. 29 Oct. 2013. *YouTube*. Web. 24 Feb. 2017. <https://www.youtube.com/watch?v=BMmNKYrp-4U>.

Free Books by Charles River Editors

We have brand new titles available for free most days of the week. To see which of our titles are currently free, click on this link.

Discounted Books by Charles River Editors

We have titles at a discount price of just 99 cents everyday. To see which of our titles are currently 99 cents, click on this link.

Printed in Great Britain
by Amazon